Contents

art boy way draw can keep
know better good pretty after when

A **Listen and repeat.**   **B** **Read, trace, and write.** T1

1.

art
_____

2.

boy
_____

3.

way
_____

4.

draw
_____

5.

can

can
_____

6.

keep

keep
_____

7.

know

know
_____

8.

better

better
_____

9.

good

good
_____

10.

pretty

pretty
_____

11.

after

after
_____

12.

when

when
_____

C Read and count.

pretty
better
good
good
good
good
pretty
better
good
good
better

better ☐

good ☐

pretty ☐

D Listen and number.   E Listen, point, and read.

☐

Olivia is a pretty girl.

☐ ☐

Now she can sing better.

☐

Jason is a handsome boy.

☐ ☐

He draws after school.

Singing Better

Olivia is a pretty girl.

She likes to sing.

The problem is that she is not a good singer.

She wants to sing better.

Olivia's mom takes her to a singing academy.
"Open your mouth when you are singing.
Sing with energy, Olivia!"

Olivia sings on her way to school.

She sings after school.

She sings at night.

Olivia keeps practicing.

Now she can sing better.

Jason is a handsome boy.

He likes to draw.

The problem is that he is not a good artist.

He wants to draw better.

Jason's mom takes him to an art academy.
"Start with basic shapes. Draw what you see,
not what you know, Jason!"

Jason draws during recess at school.

He draws after school.

He draws at night.

Jason keeps drawing.

Now he can draw better.

Activities

T3

A Write, match, and read.

1.
2.
3.
4.

b ☐☐   a ☐☐   dr ☐☐   w ☐☐

•   •   •   •

•   •   •   •

aw   rt   oy   ay

B Read, circle, and write.

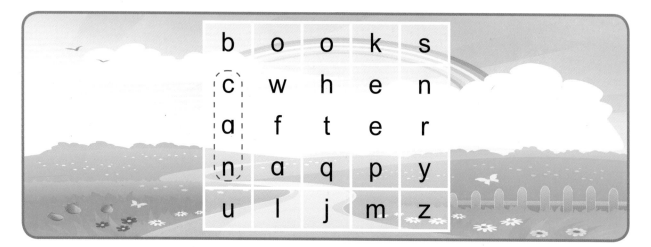

1. can _____
2. keep _____
3. when _____
4. after _____

C Fill in the blanks and find a word.

1.

2.

3.

 = _____

D Place the stickers and write. ❶

1.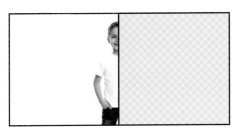

_____

2.

_____

3.

_____

4.

_____

E Listen, repeat and check three times.

F Read on your own and check 😊 or 🙁.

Can you read?

1. pretty ⬜⬜⬜   Olivia is a pretty girl.   😊 🙁

2. want ⬜⬜⬜   She wants to sing better.   😊 🙁

3. academy ⬜⬜⬜   Olivia's mom takes her to a singing academy.   😊 🙁

4. sing ⬜⬜⬜   She sings after school.   😊 🙁

5. can ⬜⬜⬜   Now she can sing better.   😊 🙁

6. boy ⬜⬜⬜   Jason is a handsome boy.   😊 🙁

7. draw ⬜⬜⬜   He wants to draw better.   😊 🙁

8. art ⬜⬜⬜   Jason's mom takes him to an art academy.   😊 🙁

9. after ⬜⬜⬜   He draws after school.   😊 🙁

10. better ⬜⬜⬜   Now he can draw better.   😊 🙁

G Look, read, and stick. ❷

1.

Olivia is a ⬜⬜⬜ girl.

2.

She wants to sing ⬜⬜⬜ .

3.

She sings ⬜⬜⬜ school.

4.

Jason is a handsome ⬜⬜⬜ .

5.

He wants to ⬜⬜⬜ better.

6.

Now he ⬜⬜⬜ draw better.

ball children fly up came got
put was wish only but the

A **Listen and repeat.** **B** **Read, trace, and write.**   T5

1.

ball
_____
- - - - - - - -
_____

2.

children
_____
- - - - - - - -
_____

3.

fly
_____
- - - - - - - -
_____

4.

up
_____
- - - - - - - -
_____

5.

came

came
_____
- - - - - - - -
_____

6.

got

got
_____
- - - - - - - -
_____

7.

put

put
_____
- - - - - - - -
_____

8.

was

was
_____
- - - - - - - -
_____

9.

wish

wish
_____
- - - - - - - -
_____

10.

only

only
_____
- - - - - - - -
_____

11.

but

but
_____
- - - - - - - -
_____

12.

the

the
_____
- - - - - - - -
_____

C Look and draw.

was   came   fly

was   (fly) came   came

came   was   fly

fly	=	○
was	=	△
came	=	□

D Listen and number.

E Listen, point, and read.

☐ ☐

"I wish I could fly to the stars!"

☐☐

He put up a poster to find some friends.

☐

"You need to be the best at something."

☐ ☐

Many children came to join the trip.

A Trip to the Stars

Mike loved to look at the stars.

"I wish I could fly to the stars!"

Mike decided to build a rocket to visit the stars.

It took him months to build the rocket.

He was ready to travel, but he did not want to go alone. He put up a poster to find some friends.

There was only one requirement to join.

"You need to be the best at something."

Many children came to join the trip.

Mike asked them how they were the best.

"Hi, I am Tom. I am the fastest runner in my class." Tom got on.

"Hello, I am Nora. I am the tallest
in my class." Nora got on.

"Hi, I am Sean. I can juggle the most balls in my class." Sean got on.

"Hello, I am Emily. I have the longest hair in my class." Emily got on.

Mike, Tom, Nora, Sean, and Emily got on the rocket. They took off to travel to the stars!

Activities

A Connect, trace, and write.

1.
   but — — — — — — —

2. q c t
   g o d
   got — — — — — — —

3. o n r j
   s e l y
   only — — — — — — —

B Fill in the blanks and write a word.

1.

2.

3.

4.

＝ — — — — — — —

C. Listen, circle, and write.

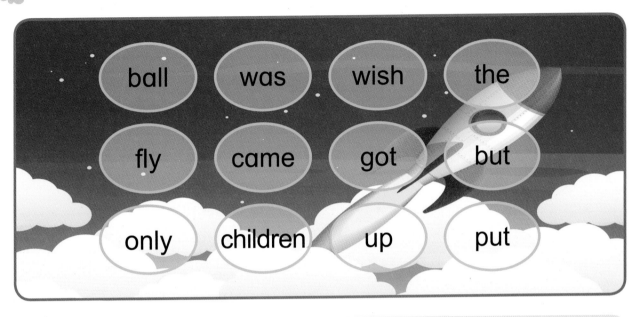

ball · was · wish · the
fly · came · got · but
only · children · up · put

1. "I _____ I could fly to the stars!"

2. He _____ up a poster to find some friends.

3. Many children _____ to join the trip.

D. Read and place the stickers.

1. "I wish I could _____ to the stars!"

2. "You need to be _____ best at something."

3. "I can juggle the most _____ s in my class."

E Listen, repeat and check three times.

F Read on your own and check 😊 or ☹️.

Can you read?

1. wish ☐☐☐ "I wish I could fly to the stars!"

2. rocket ☐☐☐ Mike decided to build a rocket to visit the stars.

3. put ☐☐☐ He put up a poster to find some friends.

4. the ☐☐☐ "You need to be the best at something."

5. children ☐☐☐ Many children came to join the trip.

6. class ☐☐☐ "I am the fastest runner in my class."

7. tallest ☐☐☐ "I am the tallest in my class."

8. ball ☐☐☐ "I can juggle the most balls in my class."

9. longest ☐☐☐ "I have the longest hair in my class."

10. star ☐☐☐ They took off to travel to the stars!

G **Read and place the stickers. Write the words.** ❷

I   1.   I could   2.   to the stars!

I decided to build a rocket to visit the stars.

It took me months to build the rocket.

I am ready to travel,   3.   I don't want to go alone.

I want to find some friends.

There is   4.   one requirement to join.

"You need to be the best at something."

1. _____ _____ _____

2. _____ _____ _____

3. _____ _____ _____

4. _____ _____ _____

baby bird nest cut sleep wash
pick shall will going own this

A Listen and repeat. **B** Read, trace, and write. T9

1.
baby
_____

2.
bird
_____

3.
nest
_____

4.
cut
_____

5.
sleep
_____

6.
wash
_____

7.
pick
pick
_____

8.
shall
shall
_____

9.
will
will
_____

10.
going
going
_____

11.
own
own
_____

12.
this
this
_____

C Find, match the color, and write.

this	will	shall
this	will	this
will	this	shall
this	will	shall
this	shall	

this	will	shall
this		

D Listen and number.   ## E Listen, point, and read.

☐

Julia is going on a picnic tomorrow.

☐   ☐

"Mom, I want to make my own lunch!"

☐   ☐

"First, you must pick which bread to use."

☐

"Next, you must cut the tomato into slices."

My Own Lunch

Julia is going on a picnic tomorrow.

This is the first picnic since her baby brother was born.

"Mom, I want to make my own lunch!" Julia says.
"Okay. You can make your own. I will help you,"
Mom says.

The next morning, Julia wakes up early.

"You must wash your hands," Mom smiles.

"First, you must pick which bread to use."

"I will use this bagel."

"Great! Next, you must cut the tomato into slices. Please be careful when you cut it."

"What shall I do next, Mom?"
"Spread mayo on the bagel and then put lettuce on it."

"Then, add ham and the sliced tomato on top."

"Finally, I will add the other half of the bagel on top of it. Yeah! I made my own bagel sandwich."

Julia, her baby brother, and her mom and dad are going to the park. Her baby brother is sleeping on a blanket.

A bird is singing in its nest.

Julia is playing with other children at the park.

It is lunch time. Julia can't wait to have her own sandwich. "Mom, this is really delicious," Julia shouts with joy.

Activities

 A **Write, match, and read.**

1.

2.

3.

4.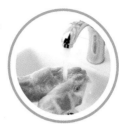

b ⬜⬜⬜   b ⬜⬜⬜   c ⬜⬜   w ⬜⬜⬜

•   •   •   •

•   •   •   •

ut   aby   ash   ird

 B **Look, circle, and write.**

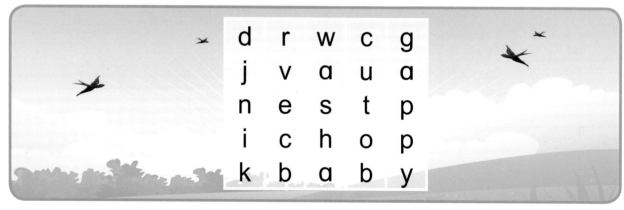

d	r	w	c	g
j	v	a	u	a
n	e	s	t	p
i	c	h	o	p
k	b	a	b	y

1.  _____

2. _____

3.  _____

4.  _____

C Fill in the blanks and find a word.

1.

2.

3.

4.

_____ = _____

D Place the stickers and circle. ①

1. | l | l   will   shall

2. p   baby   pick

3. p   sleep   nest

4. g | o   bird   going

E Listen, repeat and check three times.

F Read on your own and check 😊 or ☹ .

Can you read?

1. going ☐☐☐ Julia is going on a picnic tomorrow. 😊 ☹

2. own ☐☐☐ "Mom, I want to make my own lunch!" 😊 ☹

3. next ☐☐☐ The next morning, Julia wakes up early. 😊 ☹

4. pick ☐☐☐ "First, you must pick which bread to use." 😊 ☹

5. cut ☐☐☐ "Next, you must cut the tomato into slices." 😊 ☹

6. spread ☐☐☐ "Spread mayo on the bagel and then put lettuce on it." 😊 ☹

7. add ☐☐☐ "Add ham and the sliced tomato on top." 😊 ☹

8. baby ☐☐☐ Her baby brother is sleeping on a blanket. 😊 ☹

9. park ☐☐☐ Julia is playing with other children at the park. 😊 ☹

10. this ☐☐☐ "This is really delicious." 😊 ☹

G **Look, follow, and write.**

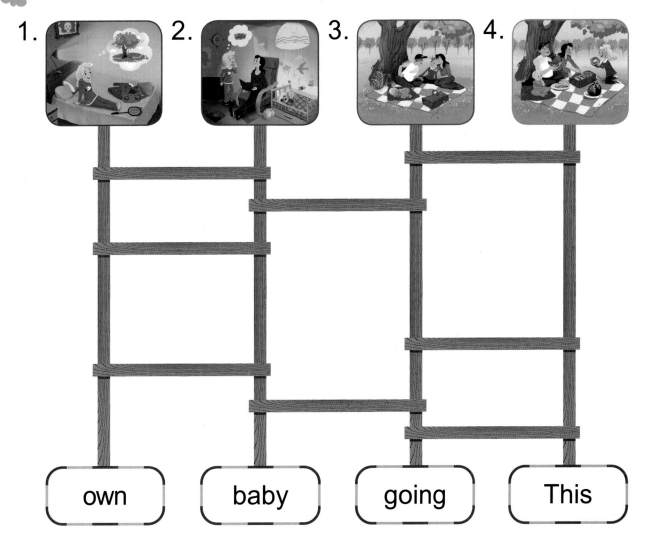

1. Julia is _____ on a picnic tomorrow.

2. "Mom, I want to make my _____ lunch!"

3. Her _____ brother is sleeping on a blanket.

4. "_____ is really delicious."

hill paper stick water fun again
much out please small an under

A Listen and repeat. **B** Read, trace, and write. T13

1.

hill
_____

2.

paper
_____

3.

stick
_____

4.

water
_____

5. fun

fun
_____

6. again

again
_____

7. much

much
_____

8. out

out
_____

9. please

please
_____

10. small

small
_____

11. an

an
_____

12. under

under
_____

C Find, circle, and count.

1. | an | oninanentheanbeanmensand | ☐ |

2. | out | southousemouseaboutmount | ☐ |

3. | again | trwagainstwistagainydagain | ☐ |

4. | paper | popcorpaperatiopapoqpapers | ☐ |

D Listen and number.   E Listen, point, and read.

☐

He walks up the hill with his friends.

☐

"Drop some colored water on each square."

☐

"The part under the plastic square is dry."

☐ ☐

"I had so much fun today, and I learned something!"

Story **Evan's First Day**

Evan is excited to start a new school year.

He wants to see his friends again.

Evan's school is on a hill.

He walks up the hill with his friends.

Evan's favorite subject is science.

Mr. Jones, the science teacher, comes in the

class.

"Today, we will do an interesting experiment."
He hands out two small squares and a piece
of paper to each student.

One square is plastic. The other square is cloth.
On each table there is a bowl of colored water.
There are four sticks, too.

"Please put the squares on the paper.
Drop some colored water on each square."

"Now look under the squares at the paper. Which part of the paper is dry? That is right. The part under the plastic square is dry."

"Coated nylon is very similar to plastic.
That is why raincoats are made of coated
nylon."

"How was your first day of school, Evan?"
"I had so much fun today, and I learned
something, Mom!"

"Glad to hear that. What did you learn?"

"I learned why raincoats are not made of cloth!"

Evan smiles back.

Activities

A Connect, trace, and write.

1.
f	o	n
m	u	z

fun _____

2.
n	m	d	u	p
u	n	b	e	r

under _____

3.
a	j	a	i	r
b	g	s	o	n

again _____

B Fill in the blanks and write a word.

1.

2.

3.

4.

 Glad to hear .

C Read and draw.

much = △ small = ○ under = □ please = ☆

much	under	please	small
under	much	under	please
please	much	please	small
small	please	much	under

D Listen, circle, and place the stickers.

1. | hill | small |

h	

2. | fun | out |

o	

3. | paper | water |

	ter

4. | stick | again |

	ick

E Listen, repeat and check three times.

F Read on your own and check 😊 or 🙁 .

Can you read?

1. excited ☐☐☐
Evan is excited to start a new school year.

2. hill ☐☐☐
He walks up the hill with his friends.

3. science ☐☐☐
Evan's favorite subject is science.

4. small ☐☐☐
Mr. Jones hands out two small squares and a piece of paper.

5. square ☐☐☐
One square is plastic. The other square is cloth.

6. water ☐☐☐
"Drop some colored water on each square."

7. under ☐☐☐
"The part under the plastic square is dry."

8. raincoat ☐☐☐
"That is why raincoats are made of coated nylon."

9. much ☐☐☐
"I had so much fun today, and I learned something!"

10. learn ☐☐☐
"I learned why raincoats are not made of cloth!"

G Look, number, and stick. ❷

"I had so ____ fun today, and I learned something!"

Evan is ____ to start a new school year.

He walks up the ____ with his friends.

"That is why ____s are made of coated nylon."

"I ____ed why raincoats are not made of cloth!"

"The part ____ the plastic square is dry."

Review

 Check the words you can read.

☐ after	☐ children	☐ nest	☐ stick
☐ again	☐ cut	☐ only	☐ the
☐ an	☐ draw	☐ out	☐ this
☐ art	☐ fly	☐ own	☐ under
☐ baby	☐ fun	☐ paper	☐ up
☐ ball	☐ going	☐ pick	☐ was
☐ better	☐ good	☐ please	☐ wash
☐ bird	☐ got	☐ pretty	☐ water
☐ boy	☐ hill	☐ put	☐ way
☐ but	☐ keep	☐ shall	☐ when
☐ came	☐ know	☐ sleep	☐ will
☐ can	☐ much	☐ small	☐ wish

Break the code. Use the numbers to find out each word.

What can you do?

o	a	N	m	n	e	w	d	l	y	c	s	r
1	2	3	4	5	6	7	8	9	10	11	12	13

3	1	7

9

11	2	5

13	6	2	8

4	2	5	10

					!
7	1	13	8	12	🙂

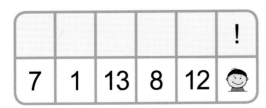

Unit 1

p. 3

C better - 3, good - 5, pretty - 2

D

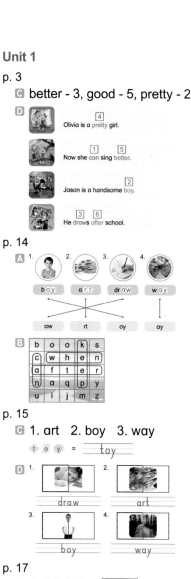

[4] Olivia is a pretty girl.

[1] [5] Now she can sing better.

[2] Jason is a handsome boy.

[3] [6] He draws after school.

p. 14

A

1. boy 2. art 3. draw 4. way

aw rt oy ay

B

b	o	o	k	s
c	w	h	e	n
a	f	t	e	r
n	a	q	p	y
u	l	j	m	z

p. 15

C 1. art 2. boy 3. way

t o y = toy

D

1. draw 2. art 3. boy 4. way

p. 17

G

1. Olivia is a pretty girl.
2. She wants to sing better.
3. She sings after school.
4. Jason is a handsome boy.
5. He wants to draw better.
6. Now he can draw better.

Unit 2

p. 19

C

fly = ○
was = △
came = □

D

[6] [1] "I wish I could fly to the stars!"

[2] [5] He put up a poster to find some friends.

[4] "You need to be the best at something."

[3] [7] Many children came to join the trip.

p. 30

A 1. n u p / b o t 2. q c t / g o d 3. o n r j / s e l y

B 1. up 2. children 3. ball 4. fly

p l a y = play

p. 31

C

ball was wish the fly came got but only children up put

1. "I wish I could fly to the stars!"
2. He put up a poster to find some friends.
3. Many children came to join the trip.

D

1. "I wish I could fly to the stars!"
2. "You need to be the best at something."
3. "I can juggle the most balls in my class."

p. 33

G 1. wish 2. fly 3. but 4. only

Unit 3

p. 35

C

	this	will	shall
	this		shall
	this	will	
	this	will	shall
		will	
	this		shall

D

[3] Julia is going on a picnic tomorrow.

[6] [2] "Mom, I want to make my own lunch!"

[1] [4] "First, you must pick which bread to use."

[5] "Next, you must cut the tomato into slices."

p. 46

A

1. baby 2. bird 3. cut 4. wash

ut aby ash ird

B

d	r	w	c	g
j	v	a	u	a
n	e	s	t	p
i	c	h	o	p
k	b	a	b	y

1. nest 2. baby 3. cut 4. wash

p. 47

C 1. cut 2. wash 3. bird 4. nest

t h i s = this

D

1. w i l l (will) shall
2. p i c k baby (pick)
3. s l e e p (sleep) nest
4. g o i n g bird (going)

p. 49

G

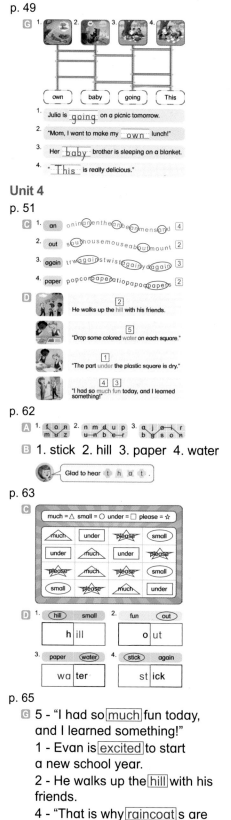

1. 2. 3. 4.

own baby going This

1. Julia is going on a picnic tomorrow.
2. "Mom, I want to make my own lunch!"
3. Her baby brother is sleeping on a blanket.
4. "This is really delicious."

Unit 4

p. 51

C

1. an oninonenthonbeonmensand [4]
2. out southousemouseaboutmount [2]
3. again trwoagainstwistagainyagain [3]
4. paper popcompaperatiopapoapapers [2]

D

[2] He walks up the hill with his friends.

[5] "Drop some colored water on each square."

[1] "The part under the plastic square is dry."

[4] [3] "I had so much fun today, and I learned something!"

p. 62

A 1. f o n / m u z 2. n m d u p / u n b e r 3. a j a i r / b g s o n

B 1. stick 2. hill 3. paper 4. water

Glad to hear t h a t

p. 63

C

much = △ small = ○ under = □ please = ☆

much	under	please	small
under	much	under	please
please	much	please	small
small	please	much	under

D

1. (hill) small → h ill
2. fun (out) → o ut
3. paper (water) → wa ter
4. (stick) again → st ick

p. 65

G 5 - "I had so much fun today, and I learned something!"

1 - Evan is excited to start a new school year.

2 - He walks up the hill with his friends.

4 - "That is why raincoats are made of coated nylon."

6 - "I learned why raincoats are not made of cloth!"

3 - "The part under the plastic square is dry."

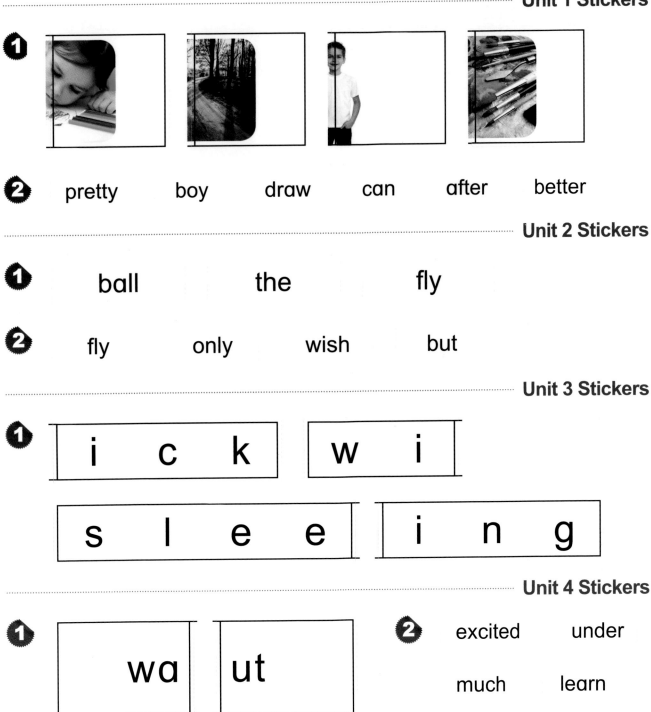

❶

❷ pretty   boy   draw   can   after   better

❶ ball   the   fly

❷ fly   only   wish   but

❶

| i | c | k |

| w | i |

| s | l | e | e |

| i | n | g |

❶

wa

ut

ill

st

❷ excited   under

much   learn

hill   raincoat